The History

A Mediterranean Gem
of History and Culture

Copyright © 2023 by Nuria Rehn and Einar Felix Hansen.

All rights reserved. No part of this publication may be reproduced, stored in a retrieval system, or transmitted, in any form or by any means, electronic, mechanical, photocopying, recording, or otherwise, without the prior written permission of the copyright holder. This book was created with the help of Artificial Intelligence technology.

The contents of this book are intended for entertainment purposes only. While every effort has been made to ensure the accuracy and reliability of the information presented, the author and publisher make no warranties or representations as to the accuracy, completeness, or suitability of the information contained herein. The information presented in this book is not intended as a substitute for professional advice, and readers should consult with qualified professionals in the relevant fields for specific advice.

The Jewel of the Mediterranean: Introduction to Malta 6

A Glimpse into Prehistoric Malta: The Megalithic Temples 10

The Phoenician Legacy: Malta's Ancient Connections 13

Rome's Mediterranean Outpost: Malta during the Roman Era 16

The Byzantine Influence: Malta in Late Antiquity 19

Arab Rule and the Islamic Influence on Malta 22

Norman Conquests and the Arrival of the Knights Templar 25

The Knights of St. John: Malta's Golden Age 28

The Great Siege of Malta: Withstanding the Ottoman Empire 31

The Knights' Legacy: Architecture and Fortifications 34

The French Interlude: Malta under Napoleon Bonaparte 37

British Rule and the Strategic Importance of Malta 39

The Maltese Uprising: Nationalism and Independence 42

Post-Independence Challenges: Building a Modern Nation 45

Malta in World War II: The Island's Heroic Resistance 48

Maltese Culture and Identity: Language, Customs, and Traditions 51

Exploring Malta's Countryside: Nature and Wildlife 54

The Azure Window and Natural Wonders of Malta 57

Maltese Cuisine: A Fusion of Mediterranean Flavors 60

The Maltese Language: A Unique Semitic Hybrid 63

Valletta: The Fortress City and UNESCO World Heritage Site 66

Mdina: The Silent City of Malta 69

The Three Cities: Vittoriosa, Senglea, and Cospicua 72

The Hypogeum of Hal-Saflieni: An Ancient Underground Temple 75

Gozo: The Sister Island of Maltese Legends 78

The Blue Grotto and the Mysteries of the Sea 81

St. John's Co-Cathedral: Baroque Splendor in Valletta 84

The Malta Experience: A Multimedia Journey through History 87

The Malta Maritime Museum: Tales of the Sea 90

From Megaliths to Modernity: Malta's Enduring Legacy 93

Conclusion 96

The Jewel of the Mediterranean: Introduction to Malta

Nestled in the heart of the Mediterranean Sea lies the archipelago of Malta, a small yet captivating group of islands that has captured the imagination of travelers for centuries. Renowned for its rich history, vibrant culture, and stunning natural beauty, Malta stands as a jewel in the Mediterranean, enticing visitors from all corners of the globe.

Malta, comprising three main islands - Malta, Gozo, and Comino - boasts a strategic location at the crossroads of Europe, Africa, and the Middle East. Its central position has made it a coveted territory throughout history, attracting various civilizations and shaping its unique identity.

The earliest evidence of human habitation in Malta dates back to around 5200 BCE, making it one of the oldest inhabited regions in the world. The islands have witnessed the rise and fall of numerous civilizations, each leaving an indelible mark on the cultural tapestry of Malta.

One of the most remarkable aspects of Malta's history is its megalithic temples. Dating back to 3600 BCE, these ancient structures predate the Egyptian pyramids and Stonehenge, making them some of the oldest freestanding structures on Earth. The temples, such as Ġgantija and Ħaġar Qim, showcase the remarkable engineering skills and spiritual beliefs of the island's early inhabitants.

Throughout antiquity, Malta played a pivotal role in maritime trade routes, attracting the attention of powerful civilizations. The Phoenicians, renowned seafarers and traders, established a presence on the islands around the 8th century BCE, followed by the Carthaginians and eventually the Romans.

Under Roman rule, Malta flourished as a prosperous outpost of the empire. The Romans constructed grand villas, bathhouses, and roads, leaving behind an architectural legacy that still resonates today. Remnants of Roman settlements and artifacts can be explored in sites like the Roman Domus in Rabat and the Roman Villa in Żejtun.

In the 4th century CE, Malta fell under Byzantine rule, marking a period of significant cultural and religious influence. Christianity spread across the islands, leaving behind awe-inspiring catacombs and basilicas, testaments to the early Christian community's devotion.

The Arab conquest of Malta in 870 CE introduced Islamic influences, adding another layer to the island's diverse heritage. The Arabs brought advancements in agriculture, trade, and language, shaping Malta's evolution and leaving traces that can still be discerned today.

One of the pivotal chapters in Malta's history unfolded with the arrival of the Knights of St. John in the 16th century. Seeking refuge after the loss of Rhodes, the Knights established their headquarters on the island and transformed Malta into a formidable fortress. Their rule, known as the Order of St. John, ushered in an era of splendor and cultural refinement.

The Knights' most defining moment came in 1565 during the Great Siege of Malta, a legendary battle against the

Ottoman Empire. Despite being vastly outnumbered, the Knights and the local Maltese population valiantly defended the islands, repelling the invaders and solidifying Malta's reputation as an impregnable stronghold.

The Great Siege cemented Malta's place in history, attracting admiration and respect from neighboring powers. As a testament to their gratitude, the Knights embellished Malta with magnificent palaces, churches, and fortifications, notably the grand fortress city of Valletta. Designed by the eminent architect Francesco Laparelli and later completed by Girolamo Cassar, Valletta became a UNESCO World Heritage Site in 1980, renowned for its fortified walls, palaces, and awe-inspiring St. John's Co-Cathedral.

The 19th century saw a shift in Malta's political landscape when the islands came under British rule. The strategic importance of Malta as a naval base during the height of the British Empire brought significant developments, including the construction of the Grand Harbor and the Malta Dockyard.

Throughout the 20th century, Malta faced challenges and transformations. In World War II, the islands endured relentless bombings and a prolonged siege, earning the George Cross, a prestigious civilian award, for their bravery and resilience. Post-war, Malta embarked on a path towards self-governance and ultimately achieved independence from British colonial rule in 1964.

Today, Malta stands as a proud member of the European Union, embracing its multicultural heritage and fostering a vibrant modern society. The Maltese language, a unique Semitic hybrid infused with Latin, influences from neighboring Mediterranean languages, and English, serves as a testament to the island's diverse linguistic heritage.

Beyond its captivating history, Malta's natural beauty entices visitors from around the world. Its rugged coastline boasts breathtaking cliffs, secluded coves, and enchanting azure waters. The Blue Grotto, a system of sea caves, and the pristine beaches of Golden Bay and Ramla Bay are just a few of the island's natural wonders.

Additionally, the Maltese archipelago is home to a rich array of flora and fauna. Despite its small size, Malta boasts an impressive diversity of endemic plant species, such as the Maltese rock-centaury and the Maltese pyramidal orchid. The islands also provide crucial habitats for migratory birds and serve as breeding grounds for species like the Cory's shearwater and the European storm petrel.

In the next chapters, we will delve deeper into Malta's ancient and medieval history, exploring the legacy of the Knights of St. John, the intricacies of Maltese culture, the enchanting sights of Valletta and Mdina, and the untamed beauty of Gozo. Together, let us embark on a captivating journey through the fascinating history of Malta, unearthing the secrets and treasures that make it truly the Jewel of the Mediterranean.

A Glimpse into Prehistoric Malta: The Megalithic Temples

Deep in the annals of time, on the picturesque islands of Malta, a remarkable chapter in human history unfolded. The prehistoric era of Malta, spanning from around 5200 BCE to 2500 BCE, witnessed the construction of extraordinary megalithic temples that continue to astound and intrigue archaeologists and visitors alike.

These megalithic temples, a testament to the ingenuity and skill of our ancestors, represent some of the oldest freestanding stone structures in the world. They predate even the magnificent pyramids of Egypt and the iconic Stonehenge, offering a fascinating glimpse into the lives and beliefs of Malta's earliest inhabitants.

The temples are scattered across the islands of Malta and Gozo, each with its own unique character and architectural style. The most renowned and well-preserved of these temples include Ġgantija, Ħaġar Qim, Mnajdra, Tarxien, and Ħal Saflieni Hypogeum, all of which have been recognized as UNESCO World Heritage Sites.

Ġgantija, located on the island of Gozo, is one of the most remarkable megalithic temple complexes in existence. Dating back to approximately 3600 BCE, Ġgantija's temples are composed of massive limestone blocks, some weighing over 50 tons. The name Ġgantija, derived from the Maltese word for "giant," alludes to the awe-inspiring size and scale of these structures.

The temples of Ħaġar Qim and Mnajdra, situated on the southern coast of Malta, exemplify the intricate craftsmanship and spiritual significance of the megalithic temples. Built using the same massive limestone blocks, these temples were meticulously aligned with celestial phenomena, such as the solstices and equinoxes, showcasing the early inhabitants' profound connection to the cosmos.

At Tarxien, located in southeastern Malta, a complex of four temples bears witness to the evolution of temple architecture throughout the prehistoric period. Intricate carvings and decorations, including spirals, animals, and fertility symbols, adorn the temple walls, providing invaluable insights into the religious and cultural practices of Malta's ancient inhabitants.

One of the most enigmatic and captivating sites in Malta is the Ħal Saflieni Hypogeum, an underground temple complex situated in the town of Paola. Discovered in 1902, the Hypogeum is a subterranean sanctuary carved into the bedrock, consisting of interconnected chambers and passageways. It is believed to have served as a burial site, as well as a place of worship and ritual ceremonies.

The megalithic temples of Malta were not merely architectural marvels; they were also sacred spaces where rituals, ceremonies, and communal gatherings took place. Archaeological excavations have unearthed pottery, figurines, tools, and human remains within the temple complexes, shedding light on the customs, beliefs, and daily lives of Malta's ancient inhabitants.

The construction of these temples was a monumental feat, requiring immense communal effort and skilled craftsmanship. The transportation and positioning of colossal stone blocks, the precise alignment with celestial events, and the intricate detailing all attest to the advanced engineering knowledge and social organization of the prehistoric Maltese society.

Despite the passage of millennia, the megalithic temples of Malta have endured the tests of time, standing as enduring symbols of our shared human heritage. They offer a tantalizing glimpse into the mysteries of our past, sparking questions about the purpose, symbolism, and significance of these awe-inspiring structures.

The Phoenician Legacy: Malta's Ancient Connections

In the vast tapestry of Malta's rich history, the Phoenician legacy stands as a significant chapter that connects this Mediterranean archipelago to the ancient world. The Phoenicians, renowned seafarers and traders, left an indelible mark on Malta's cultural landscape, forging lasting connections that shaped the island's development.

Originating from the eastern shores of the Mediterranean, the Phoenicians were a Semitic people who established a network of colonies and trading outposts across the Mediterranean basin. Their seafaring prowess and commercial acumen propelled them to become a dominant force in maritime trade during the first millennium BCE.

Around the 8th century BCE, the Phoenicians set their sights on Malta, recognizing its strategic position along the sea routes linking the eastern and western Mediterranean. The allure of its natural harbors and fertile land made Malta an ideal stopover for their ships, enabling them to replenish supplies and conduct trade with neighboring regions.

The Phoenicians established a presence on the islands, particularly in areas such as modern-day Marsaxlokk and Mellieħa, where evidence of Phoenician settlements and artifacts have been uncovered. These settlements served as important trading hubs, facilitating the exchange of goods and ideas between the Phoenicians and other Mediterranean civilizations.

One of the enduring legacies of the Phoenician presence in Malta is the impact on language and culture. The Phoenician language, a Semitic tongue closely related to Hebrew and Aramaic, left traces in the Maltese language, influencing its vocabulary and structure. The Maltese alphabet, derived from the Latin script, also incorporates some Phoenician letter forms, further attesting to this linguistic connection.

Trade played a central role in the Phoenician-Maltese relationship. The Phoenicians, known for their maritime expertise, brought goods from far-flung regions, including precious metals, exotic spices, textiles, and luxury items. In exchange, Malta offered its agricultural produce, such as grain, olive oil, and wine, which were highly sought after commodities in the ancient Mediterranean world.

The Phoenician legacy in Malta is not limited to economic ties; it also encompasses religious and cultural influences. The Phoenicians worshipped a pantheon of deities, with Baal, Astarte, and Melqart among the most prominent. Their religious practices, characterized by rituals, sacrifices, and reverence for nature, found resonance in Malta's spiritual beliefs, leaving an imprint on the island's religious customs.

Archaeological excavations have revealed Phoenician sanctuaries, votive offerings, and inscriptions on the islands, providing valuable insights into their religious practices. The discovery of the Phoenician stela at Tas-Silġ in Marsaxlokk, a sacred stone slab with an inscription dedicated to the Phoenician god Melqart, further underscores the enduring spiritual connections between Malta and the Phoenician world.

The Phoenician legacy in Malta continued to thrive even after their direct presence waned. As other civilizations rose to prominence, notably the Carthaginians and the Romans, Malta maintained its commercial ties and cultural exchange with the wider Mediterranean world, with Phoenician influences permeating the fabric of Maltese society.

Today, the Phoenician legacy lives on in the collective memory of the Maltese people and in the archaeological remains that bear witness to this ancient connection. The enduring impact of Phoenician trade, language, and religious practices serves as a testament to the cultural intermingling and the cross-pollination of ideas that have shaped Malta's historical trajectory.

Rome's Mediterranean Outpost: Malta during the Roman Era

During the expansive reign of the Roman Empire, Malta emerged as a strategic Mediterranean outpost, playing a crucial role in Rome's imperial ambitions. The Roman era in Malta, which spanned from 218 BCE to the 4th century CE, brought significant developments, leaving an indelible mark on the islands' history and culture.

The Roman presence in Malta began with the First Punic War when the islands were annexed by Rome from the Carthaginians in 218 BCE. The strategic location of Malta, situated between Sicily and North Africa, made it an advantageous naval base for the Roman forces.

Under Roman rule, Malta experienced a period of stability and prosperity. The Romans introduced various infrastructural improvements, transforming Malta into a thriving hub of commerce and trade. They constructed grand villas, bathhouses, aqueducts, and roads, which enhanced the quality of life and facilitated the movement of goods and people across the islands.

One notable legacy of the Roman era in Malta is the extensive road network that crisscrossed the islands. These well-paved roads, built with durable materials such as limestone and basalt, connected major settlements and allowed for efficient transportation and communication. The most famous of these roads, the Via Appia, connected the capital city of Melite (modern-day Mdina) to the eastern coast of the island.

Roman influence is also evident in the architectural styles that emerged during this period. Roman villas, characterized by their spacious layouts, courtyards, and intricate mosaic floors, dotted the Maltese landscape. The Roman Domus in Rabat, a well-preserved example of a Roman townhouse, showcases the opulence and refinement of Roman architectural design.

Religious practices underwent transformations during the Roman era in Malta. The Romans, with their polytheistic beliefs, brought their pantheon of gods and goddesses to the islands. Temples dedicated to deities such as Jupiter, Juno, and Minerva were erected, fusing Roman religious customs with pre-existing Maltese beliefs. The remains of Roman temples, such as the Roman Villa in Żejtun, provide glimpses into the syncretism of these religious traditions.

Roman Malta also witnessed the spread of Christianity, which gained prominence during the later years of Roman rule. The Apostle Paul, traditionally believed to have shipwrecked on the island, brought Christianity to Malta in the 1st century CE. The catacombs of St. Paul's and St. Agatha's in Rabat serve as testament to the early Christian community and their burial practices.

Trade flourished under Roman administration, with Malta serving as a vital commercial crossroads. The islands' strategic location, coupled with the Roman Empire's vast network of trade routes, facilitated the exchange of goods and ideas. Malta became a hub for the import and export of commodities such as olive oil, wine, grain, and pottery, connecting the islands to the wider Mediterranean economy.

The Roman era in Malta was not without its challenges. The islands experienced periodic invasions and raids, particularly by Barbary pirates and other Mediterranean powers vying for control. However, Malta's strategic fortifications and the presence of Roman legions stationed on the islands bolstered its defenses and deterred potential threats.

As the Roman Empire declined and faced internal turmoil, Malta witnessed a shift in political power. The Byzantine Empire, the successor to the Eastern Roman Empire, eventually assumed control of the islands in the 6th century CE, ushering in a new era in Malta's history.

The Roman era in Malta left an enduring imprint on the islands' culture, infrastructure, and religious practices. The legacy of Roman architectural design, engineering prowess, and trade networks enriched the Maltese society, intertwining it with the broader tapestry of the Roman Empire.

The Byzantine Influence: Malta in Late Antiquity

In the shifting tides of history, Malta witnessed the rise of the Byzantine Empire, which left an indelible mark on the islands during the Late Antiquity period. The Byzantine influence on Malta, spanning from the 6th to the 9th century CE, brought significant political, cultural, and religious transformations to this Mediterranean archipelago.

Following the fall of the Western Roman Empire, Malta came under the dominion of the Byzantine Empire, the eastern half of the Roman Empire that endured and flourished for centuries. Under Byzantine rule, Malta became part of the Exarchate of Africa, which encompassed territories across North Africa and the central Mediterranean region.

The Byzantines brought administrative reforms and governance structures that reshaped Malta's political landscape. The island became a province under the Byzantine Exarchate, with a centralized administration and a hierarchical system of local governance. The governor, known as the comes, oversaw the day-to-day affairs of the island, ensuring the enforcement of imperial policies and the collection of taxes.

The Byzantine influence extended beyond governance and encompassed the legal and judicial systems of Malta. Byzantine law, derived from Roman law and influenced by Christian principles, was implemented on the islands. The legal framework, with its emphasis on fairness and the protection of individual rights, served as a basis for justice and governance during this period.

Religion played a pivotal role in Byzantine Malta, as Christianity continued to flourish and evolve. The Byzantines were staunch defenders of Orthodox Christianity, and their presence reinforced the spread and consolidation of Christianity on the islands. Churches and basilicas, adorned with intricate mosaics and frescoes, emerged as centers of worship and spiritual nourishment for the growing Christian community.

One of the most significant religious developments during the Byzantine era was the construction of St. Paul's Cathedral in Mdina. Dedicated to the Apostle Paul, who was believed to have brought Christianity to Malta, the cathedral became a prominent religious and cultural symbol. Byzantine architectural influences, such as domes, arches, and decorative elements, were incorporated into the design, leaving a lasting testament to the Byzantine legacy.

Education and intellectual pursuits thrived under Byzantine rule, fostering a climate of learning and cultural exchange. The Byzantines, renowned for their preservation and transmission of ancient knowledge, brought with them a wealth of literature, philosophy, and scientific advancements. Monastic communities and scholars in Malta played a vital role in preserving and disseminating this knowledge, contributing to the intellectual vibrancy of the island.

The Byzantine era in Malta was not without challenges and external threats. The islands faced recurrent raids and invasions from Vandals, Ostrogoths, and other Mediterranean powers vying for control. The Byzantine military presence, coupled with the fortifications built during this period, helped safeguard Malta against these incursions.

The Byzantine influence gradually waned over time as the Arab conquests swept across the Mediterranean. In 870 CE, Malta fell to the Aghlabids, an Arab-Muslim dynasty. The Byzantine legacy, however, continued to reverberate in Malta's cultural, religious, and architectural fabric, leaving an enduring impact on the island's identity.

Arab Rule and the Islamic Influence on Malta

In the annals of Malta's history, the era of Arab rule stands as a significant chapter that shaped the islands and left a profound impact on their culture, language, and architectural heritage. Arab rule in Malta, which lasted from 870 to 1091 CE, brought forth a period of Islamic influence and intercultural exchange.

The Arab conquest of Malta was part of the wider expansion of the Arab-Muslim world across the Mediterranean. The Aghlabids, a dynasty based in North Africa, extended their dominion to the Maltese archipelago, establishing a presence that would endure for over two centuries.

The arrival of the Arabs marked a period of cultural and intellectual renaissance in Malta. Arab-Muslim scholars and artisans brought with them a wealth of knowledge in diverse fields, including mathematics, astronomy, medicine, and agriculture. This influx of intellectual and scientific advancements enriched Malta's cultural landscape and contributed to its overall development.

One of the most prominent contributions of Arab rule was the introduction of Islam to Malta. Mosques and Islamic institutions emerged, becoming centers of religious and educational activities. While the majority of the population remained Christian, the Islamic faith found a place within the multicultural fabric of the islands.

The Arab presence also left an indelible mark on Malta's linguistic heritage. Arabic, as the language of administration and everyday life, influenced the development of the Maltese language. Loanwords, syntax, and linguistic elements of Arabic became integrated into the evolving vernacular, shaping the unique Semitic hybrid that is the Maltese language.

The influence of Arab rule is also evident in Malta's architectural legacy. Arab architects and craftsmen introduced new construction techniques and architectural styles that fused with existing traditions. Elements such as horseshoe arches, intricately patterned decorations, and the use of local limestone can be observed in various structures across the islands, showcasing the architectural assimilation of Islamic aesthetics.

A prime example of this architectural synthesis is the medieval city of Mdina. Under Arab rule, Mdina, then known as Medina, experienced significant development and fortification. The layout of the city, its narrow winding streets, and its defensive walls were enhanced and modified to reflect the Arab influence. The mix of Arab, Norman, and medieval European architectural elements in Mdina provides a tangible testament to the intermingling of cultures during this period.

Trade and commerce flourished during Arab rule, as Malta became a hub for maritime activities in the Mediterranean. The strategic location of the islands allowed for thriving commercial exchanges between the Arab-Muslim world, Europe, and North Africa. The markets of Malta bustled with goods and commodities, facilitating economic growth and cultural exchange.

The end of Arab rule in Malta came with the Norman conquest in 1091 CE. The Normans, under the leadership of Count Roger I of Sicily, brought the islands under their control, ushering in a new era in Malta's history. However, the influence of Arab rule continued to resonate in Malta's cultural and architectural practices, contributing to its unique identity.

Norman Conquests and the Arrival of the Knights Templar

In the intricate tapestry of Malta's history, the Norman conquests and the arrival of the Knights Templar marked a transformative period that shaped the islands and set the stage for the emergence of the renowned Knights of St. John. This chapter delves into the dynamic events and influential figures that left an indelible mark on Malta during this era.

The Norman conquest of Malta took place in 1091 CE when Count Roger I of Sicily, a Norman nobleman, wrested control of the islands from Arab rule. The Normans, a people of Viking and Frankish origin, brought with them a martial spirit and a penchant for expansion.

Under Norman rule, Malta experienced a period of consolidation and stability. Count Roger I and his successors sought to strengthen their control over the islands and establish a centralized administration. They introduced feudalism, dividing the land into fiefdoms and granting estates to loyal vassals who pledged military service and allegiance.

During the Norman era, Malta became a strategic outpost in the Mediterranean. The islands' proximity to Sicily and North Africa made them vital for regional trade and as a base for naval operations. The Normans constructed fortifications and castles, such as the Cittadella in Gozo and the fortified city of Mdina, as defense against potential threats and as symbols of their power.

The Norman period also saw the arrival of religious orders, most notably the Knights Templar. The Knights Templar, a military order established in the aftermath of the First Crusade, played a significant role in the defense of Christendom and the protection of pilgrims traveling to the Holy Land. They arrived in Malta around the 12th century, establishing a presence on the islands.

The arrival of the Knights Templar brought a new dimension to Malta's religious and military landscape. The Templars, renowned for their martial skills and religious devotion, were entrusted with the defense of the Christian faith and the safeguarding of important pilgrimage routes. They established commanderies and fortified strongholds on the islands, including the commanding fortress of Fort St. Angelo.

The presence of the Knights Templar in Malta was not without controversy. Over time, the Templars accumulated vast wealth and power, which led to accusations of misconduct and heresy. In 1312, Pope Clement V disbanded the order, and their assets were transferred to the Knights Hospitaller, later known as the Knights of St. John.

The arrival of the Knights Templar set the stage for the subsequent emergence of the Knights of St. John, who would become synonymous with Malta's history and heritage. The Hospitallers, as they were also known, were originally an order dedicated to caring for the sick and injured during the Crusades. After inheriting the Templars' assets, the Hospitallers expanded their mission to include the defense of Christian territories.

The Hospitallers' presence in Malta began in 1530 when Holy Roman Emperor Charles V granted the islands to the order as a fiefdom. The Knights of St. John transformed Malta into their headquarters and embarked on a comprehensive program of fortification and urban development. The construction of the magnificent fortified city of Valletta, named after Grand Master Jean de la Valette, became their crowning achievement.

The legacy of the Norman conquests and the arrival of the Knights Templar in Malta reverberates through the centuries. The fortifications, castles, and architectural marvels that emerged during this period stand as testament to the strategic significance and enduring influence of these events. The Knights of St. John, born from this historical context, would go on to shape Malta's destiny in remarkable ways.

The Knights of St. John: Malta's Golden Age

In the vibrant tapestry of Malta's history, the era of the Knights of St. John stands as a golden age that brought prosperity, cultural refinement, and enduring architectural marvels to the islands. This chapter delves into the extraordinary legacy of the Knights of St. John and their indelible mark on Malta.

The Knights of St. John, officially known as the Sovereign Military Hospitaller Order of Saint John of Jerusalem, of Rhodes, and of Malta, emerged as a chivalric and religious order during the Crusades. Originally founded in the 11th century in Jerusalem, the order's mission encompassed caring for the sick, defending the Christian faith, and protecting pilgrims.

After the loss of their base in Rhodes to the Ottoman Empire, the Knights sought refuge and a new home. In 1530, Holy Roman Emperor Charles V granted the Maltese archipelago to the order, transforming Malta into their sovereign territory. This pivotal moment marked the beginning of a remarkable chapter in Malta's history.

Under the Knights' rule, Malta experienced a period of unrivaled splendor, cultural refinement, and prosperity. The island became a hub of Mediterranean trade, attracting merchants and craftsmen from across Europe and the Middle East. The Knights, with their vast resources and international connections, fostered an atmosphere of economic growth and cultural exchange.

One of the most iconic symbols of the Knights' presence in Malta is the city of Valletta. Constructed between 1566 and 1571 under the direction of Grand Master Jean de la Valette, Valletta was designed as a fortified city and a testament to the Knights' military prowess and architectural vision. The city's strategic layout, imposing fortifications, and grand palaces showcased the order's power and grandeur.

Valletta's architectural splendor can be witnessed in its palaces, churches, and public buildings. The Grand Master's Palace, now the seat of the President of Malta, boasts opulent interiors, stunning tapestries, and intricately decorated halls. St. John's Co-Cathedral, a masterpiece of Baroque architecture, houses awe-inspiring artistic treasures, including Caravaggio's renowned painting, "The Beheading of Saint John the Baptist."

The Knights' devotion to their religious mission is evident in the numerous churches and chapels that adorn Malta. These sacred sites, such as the Church of St. Paul's Shipwreck in Valletta and the Church of St. Lawrence in Birgu, showcase the order's spiritual commitment and the exquisite craftsmanship that went into their construction.

Beyond their military and religious duties, the Knights fostered cultural refinement and intellectual pursuits. They established libraries, academies, and schools, nurturing a climate of learning and artistic expression. The Auberge de Castille, one of the Knights' grand residences, now serves as the office of the Prime Minister and stands as a testament to their support for the arts and intellectual endeavors.

The Knights' influence extended to the rural areas of Malta, where they established agricultural estates and fortified towers. These towers, such as the iconic Red Tower in Mellieħa and the Wignacourt Tower in St. Paul's Bay, served as defensive structures and lookout points, safeguarding the islands from potential threats.

Malta's strategic position in the Mediterranean made it a target for invasion and attack. In 1565, the Knights faced their greatest challenge—the Great Siege of Malta. The Ottoman Empire, led by Sultan Suleiman the Magnificent, sought to capture the island and eradicate the Knights. Against overwhelming odds, the Knights and the Maltese people valiantly defended Malta, repelling the Ottoman forces after a grueling four-month siege. The Great Siege became a defining moment in Malta's history, cementing the reputation of the Knights as valiant defenders of Christendom.

The Knights of St. John continued to flourish in Malta for over two centuries, leaving an enduring legacy in the cultural, architectural, and social fabric of the islands. Their rule brought about an era of prosperity, artistic brilliance, and religious devotion that shaped Malta's identity and collective memory.

The Great Siege of Malta: Withstanding the Ottoman Empire

In the annals of military history, the Great Siege of Malta stands as a defining moment, showcasing the resilience and bravery of the Knights of St. John and the Maltese people against the mighty Ottoman Empire. This chapter delves into the dramatic events and extraordinary acts of heroism that unfolded during this historic siege.

The Great Siege took place in 1565, when the Ottoman Empire, under the command of Sultan Suleiman the Magnificent, set its sights on capturing Malta. The strategic importance of the island, situated at the crossroads of Europe, Africa, and the Middle East, made it a coveted prize for the Ottomans, who sought to expand their dominion.

Led by the formidable Ottoman general, Mustafa Pasha, an armada of over 200 ships and an army numbering tens of thousands descended upon Malta. The defenders of the island, consisting of around 6,000 Knights of St. John, Maltese soldiers, and local volunteers, faced overwhelming odds against this formidable force.

The siege began on May 18, 1565, and would last for four grueling months. The Ottomans unleashed a relentless bombardment of the fortifications, aiming to breach the defenses and capture key strategic positions. The defenders, however, stood firm, displaying unwavering resolve and resourcefulness in the face of overwhelming adversity.

The Knights of St. John, led by Grand Master Jean de la Valette, proved to be valiant and skilled defenders. They utilized the fortified cities of Birgu, Senglea, and the newly built Valletta as strongholds, from which they launched fierce counterattacks and repelled wave after wave of Ottoman assaults.

The Maltese people, both soldiers and civilians, played a pivotal role in the defense of their homeland. Men, women, and even children contributed to the efforts, assisting in fortification construction, providing supplies, and tending to the wounded. Their unwavering support and sacrifices demonstrated the indomitable spirit of the Maltese people.

The Ottomans, despite their superior numbers and firepower, encountered unexpected challenges during the siege. The Knights' fortifications proved to be resilient, withstanding the relentless bombardment. The arrival of reinforcements from Sicily, under the leadership of Don Garcia de Toledo, further bolstered the defenders' resolve and tilted the balance in their favor.

As the siege wore on, the defenders faced numerous hardships. Supplies dwindled, and disease ravaged the overcrowded fortifications. Yet, their determination remained unbroken. The Knights and the Maltese people fought tenaciously, repelling wave after wave of Ottoman assaults, inflicting heavy casualties on the besieging forces.

One of the most legendary episodes of the Great Siege was the heroic defense of Fort St. Elmo. This strategically vital outpost, located at the tip of the Sciberras Peninsula, held out against relentless Ottoman attacks for over a month. Despite the overwhelming odds, the defenders held their ground, buying crucial time for the rest of the island's defenses.

The turning point of the siege came on September 8, 1565, when a relief force consisting of Spanish, Sicilian, and Italian troops launched a daring amphibious assault on the Ottoman lines. This unexpected counteroffensive caught the Ottomans off guard and inflicted heavy losses. The arrival of the relief force marked a decisive moment in the siege and dealt a severe blow to the Ottoman morale.

Realizing the futility of their efforts, the Ottoman forces gradually retreated from Malta in early September 1565. The defenders had emerged victorious, their resilience and determination repelling the mighty Ottoman Empire. The Great Siege of Malta became a symbol of the indomitable spirit of the Knights of St. John and the Maltese people, inspiring future generations.

The aftermath of the Great Siege brought about a renewed sense of purpose and pride for the Knights of St. John and the people of Malta. Grand Master Jean de la Valette, who had displayed exceptional leadership and courage during the siege, became a revered figure, and the fortified city of Valletta was named in his honor.

The Great Siege of Malta remains a testament to the power of fortitude, unity, and unwavering determination in the face of overwhelming odds. It is an enduring reminder of the human spirit's ability to withstand and overcome immense challenges.

The Knights' Legacy: Architecture and Fortifications

The legacy of the Knights of St. John in Malta extends far beyond their military prowess and noble deeds. Their rule left an indelible mark on the architectural landscape of the islands, shaping the iconic forts, palaces, and fortified cities that still stand as testaments to their grandeur and engineering prowess. This chapter explores the Knights' architectural legacy and their remarkable fortifications.

During their time in Malta, the Knights of St. John undertook ambitious construction projects aimed at fortifying the island and showcasing their power and devotion. The fortified city of Valletta, their crowning achievement, stands as a UNESCO World Heritage site and a living testament to their architectural brilliance.

Valletta, founded by Grand Master Jean de la Valette and built between 1566 and 1571, is a marvel of military architecture. The city's strategic layout, fortified bastions, and imposing fortifications were meticulously designed to withstand attacks and ensure the defense of the Knights' headquarters. The majestic Grand Harbour, with its natural deep-water port, provided additional protection and facilitated maritime operations.

The fortifications of Valletta, including Fort St. Elmo, Fort St. Angelo, and Fort Tigné, were crucial elements of the city's defense system. These formidable structures were strategically positioned to guard key approaches and provide overlapping fields of fire, creating a formidable barrier against potential invaders. The forts incorporated innovative defensive features, such as bastions, curtain walls, and ravelins, which enhanced their resilience and deterrence capabilities.

Beyond Valletta, the Knights fortified other strategic locations around Malta and its sister island, Gozo. The fortified cities of Birgu (Vittoriosa), Senglea (Isla), and Mdina (the former capital) were transformed into impregnable strongholds. The fortifications of Birgu and Senglea, known as the Cottonera Lines, formed a formidable defensive system that protected the Grand Harbour and thwarted enemy incursions.

The Knights' architectural endeavors were not limited to fortifications; they also left their mark on civil and religious structures. Palaces, churches, and auberges (lodging houses) were constructed with grandeur and magnificence befitting the order's stature. The Grand Master's Palace, now the Office of the President of Malta, showcases exquisite interiors, intricate tapestries, and grand halls that reflect the opulence of the Knights' residence.

Religious architecture flourished under the Knights' patronage. St. John's Co-Cathedral in Valletta, the spiritual heart of the Knights, is a masterpiece of Baroque architecture. The cathedral's unassuming exterior belies its opulent interior, adorned with gilded sculptures, stunning frescoes, and a celebrated artistic treasure—Caravaggio's "The Beheading of Saint John the Baptist."

The legacy of the Knights' architectural prowess extends to the rural areas of Malta, where they built fortified towers and watchtowers. These structures, such as the imposing Wignacourt Tower in St. Paul's Bay and the majestic Ghajn Tuffieha Tower, served as lookout points, warning systems, and defensive strongholds, providing vital protection for the island's rural communities.

The Knights' architectural legacy is not limited to stone and mortar; it also encompasses the remarkable feats of hydraulic engineering. The Knights built an extensive system of aqueducts, underground cisterns, and wells to ensure a reliable water supply for the population and the defense of the island. The Wignacourt Aqueduct, an impressive structure spanning over 15 kilometers, stands as a testament to their mastery of water management.

The Knights' architectural achievements in Malta reflect their dedication to fortifying the island and creating a lasting legacy of military strength. Their structures harmoniously blend functionality with aesthetics, exemplifying the ideals of the Renaissance and Baroque periods.

The architectural legacy of the Knights of St. John continues to captivate visitors from around the world, who marvel at the grandeur, sophistication, and engineering ingenuity of their constructions. Their fortifications and buildings are not mere relics but living embodiments of the Knights' enduring presence and the rich historical tapestry of Malta.

The French Interlude: Malta under Napoleon Bonaparte

In the complex tapestry of Malta's history, a brief but significant chapter unfolds during the French interlude when the archipelago came under the rule of Napoleon Bonaparte. This chapter explores the events and impact of French occupation on Malta, shedding light on this transformative period.

In 1798, Napoleon Bonaparte set his sights on Malta as a strategic outpost in the Mediterranean. The Knights of St. John, whose power had waned over the years, proved unable to withstand the might of the French forces. On June 10, 1798, Napoleon's fleet arrived in Malta, marking the beginning of the French occupation.

Under French rule, significant changes took place in Malta. The Knights of St. John were expelled from the islands, and their properties were confiscated. The French established a new administration, implementing revolutionary policies and institutions.

One of the most notable actions of the French occupiers was the abolition of feudalism and the introduction of the Code Napoleon, a legal system based on equality and meritocracy. The Code Napoleon brought significant reforms to Malta's legal system, including the establishment of a civil code, the recognition of individual rights, and the uniformity of laws.

During their occupation, the French made efforts to modernize Malta's infrastructure and institutions. They initiated public works projects, such as the improvement of roads, the construction of public buildings, and the establishment of educational institutions. The University of Malta, founded in 1800, traces its roots back to this period.

Religion underwent significant changes during the French occupation. The Catholic Church, which had played a central role in Malta for centuries, faced new regulations and restrictions. The French implemented measures to secularize religious institutions, confiscating church property and asserting control over religious affairs.

The French interlude in Malta was not without resistance. The Maltese people, deeply rooted in their cultural and religious traditions, expressed discontent with the occupation. The uprising of the Maltese population against the French occupiers, known as the Maltese Uprising of 1798, became a significant moment in the struggle for independence and self-determination.

In 1800, the tide of European politics shifted, and the French forces were expelled from Malta. The British, who had been monitoring the situation closely, took control of the islands under the terms of the Treaty of Amiens.

The French interlude, although relatively short-lived, left a lasting impact on Malta. The introduction of revolutionary ideas, the modernization of institutions, and the awakening of national consciousness during this period laid the groundwork for subsequent developments in Malta's journey towards independence.

British Rule and the Strategic Importance of Malta

In the annals of Malta's history, the era of British rule stands as a significant chapter that spanned over 160 years, profoundly shaping the islands' political, social, and economic landscape. This chapter delves into the period of British rule and highlights the strategic importance of Malta in the Mediterranean.

The British took control of Malta in 1800, following the expulsion of the French forces from the islands. Under British rule, Malta became a crucial strategic outpost in the Mediterranean, serving as a naval base and a vital link between Britain and its colonies in the eastern Mediterranean and the Far East.

The strategic importance of Malta was amplified by its geographic location. Situated at the crossroads of Europe, Africa, and the Middle East, Malta offered a natural harbor, deep-water ports, and excellent anchorage, making it an ideal naval base for British operations in the region. The island's proximity to important trade routes and its potential as a refueling and resupplying station further bolstered its strategic value.

The British, recognizing Malta's strategic potential, invested heavily in fortifications and infrastructure. They expanded upon the existing fortifications built by the Knights of St. John, further strengthening Malta's defenses against potential threats. Fortifications such as Fort Ricasoli, Fort St. Elmo, and Fort St. Angelo were modernized and reinforced to safeguard the island and its naval facilities.

Under British rule, Malta experienced significant urban development and modernization. The construction of new roads, bridges, and public buildings transformed the infrastructure of the islands. Valletta, the fortified city built by the Knights of St. John, underwent further expansion and improvement, becoming a bustling administrative and commercial hub.

The strategic importance of Malta became particularly evident during the two World Wars. In World War I, Malta served as a crucial base for British operations in the Mediterranean, supporting the Allied forces in their campaigns. During World War II, Malta endured relentless aerial bombardment and sieges, earning the island the title of "The Most Bombed Place on Earth." Despite the devastation, the resilience and determination of the Maltese people and the strategic significance of the island led to its eventual victory and recognition as the "George Cross Island" for its bravery and fortitude.

The presence of the British on the islands left a lasting impact on Malta's social and cultural fabric. The English language, introduced during this period, became an official language alongside Maltese and remains widely spoken today. British institutions, including the legal system, educational system, and administrative structures, were implemented and shaped Malta's governance and society.

British rule brought about significant economic changes in Malta. The development of the island's infrastructure and the establishment of a naval base led to the growth of industries such as shipping, trade, and manufacturing. The

British also invested in the development of agriculture, improving techniques and introducing new crops, which contributed to Malta's economic diversification.

The period of British rule in Malta was not without challenges and grievances. The local population, although benefiting from the modernization efforts and economic opportunities, also faced issues of social inequality and limited political representation. However, the desire for self-governance and independence gradually gained momentum, leading to the emergence of a nationalist movement that sought to shape Malta's future.

The Maltese Uprising: Nationalism and Independence

The Maltese Uprising marked a significant turning point in Malta's history, as the archipelago embarked on a journey towards self-governance and independence. This chapter delves into the rise of nationalism and the events that unfolded during this pivotal period.

In the early 20th century, a growing sense of national identity and a desire for greater self-determination began to take hold among the Maltese population. Influenced by the ideals of democracy and the quest for independence, a nationalist movement emerged, advocating for political and social reforms.

The Maltese people sought a more active role in the governance of their homeland. As the call for self-governance grew stronger, the British colonial administration responded by gradually introducing political reforms. In 1921, Malta was granted self-government, allowing for the election of a Legislative Assembly and the appointment of a Prime Minister responsible for local affairs.

The political landscape in Malta during this period was marked by the emergence of political parties representing various ideologies and interests. The Nationalist Party, founded in 1880, became a significant force advocating for independence and the protection of Maltese interests. The party's leader, Gerald Strickland, played a pivotal role in shaping Malta's political future.

The struggle for independence faced various challenges, including the disruptions caused by World War I and World War II. During World War II, Malta endured relentless bombardment and sieges, as it became a target for Axis forces. The resilience and determination of the Maltese people, who withstood severe hardships and displayed extraordinary bravery, earned the island the prestigious George Cross.

The aftermath of World War II brought about renewed momentum for Malta's quest for independence. The Maltese population increasingly demanded self-determination and the right to shape their own destiny. Negotiations between Malta and Britain ensued, leading to the signing of the Maltese Constitution in 1964, granting the islands independence as a constitutional monarchy within the Commonwealth of Nations.

Malta's path to full independence continued to evolve, culminating in the declaration of a republic in 1974. The Republic of Malta became a sovereign nation, with a President as the head of state. This milestone solidified Malta's status as an independent nation, free to chart its own course on the global stage.

The post-independence era brought about significant changes in Malta's governance, economy, and international relations. The nation forged its own identity, focusing on strengthening democratic institutions, promoting economic growth, and cultivating international partnerships. Malta's strategic location and its commitment to neutrality enabled it to play a role in regional and global affairs.

Throughout its journey towards independence, Malta maintained strong ties with the Commonwealth and established diplomatic relations with countries around the world. The island's unique cultural heritage, linguistic diversity, and strategic location in the Mediterranean continue to shape its international standing and influence.

Post-Independence Challenges: Building a Modern Nation

The post-independence period in Malta's history presented a unique set of challenges as the nation sought to establish itself as a modern, independent entity on the global stage. This chapter delves into the diverse array of challenges faced by Malta in its journey towards building a modern nation.

Upon gaining independence in 1964 and subsequently becoming a republic in 1974, Malta faced the task of forging its own path and charting a course for its future. The nation had to address various aspects, including governance, economic development, social progress, and international relations, to build a strong foundation for a modern state.

One of the significant challenges in the post-independence era was the process of developing democratic institutions and ensuring effective governance. Malta embarked on the establishment of a robust democratic system, enshrining the principles of representative government, separation of powers, and respect for the rule of law. Political parties played a crucial role in shaping the nation's democratic landscape through elections and participatory processes.

Economic development was another paramount concern for post-independence Malta. The nation sought to diversify its economy, reduce dependence on traditional sectors, and foster sustainable growth. Initiatives were undertaken to attract foreign investments, promote entrepreneurship, and develop sectors such as tourism, financial services, manufacturing, and information technology. These efforts aimed to create employment opportunities and enhance Malta's competitiveness in the global market.

Education and human capital development emerged as essential components of building a modern nation. Malta invested in expanding access to education, improving the quality of schools and universities, and promoting research and innovation. Emphasis was placed on equipping the population with the necessary skills and knowledge to meet the demands of a rapidly changing world.

Social progress and welfare were also central to Malta's post-independence agenda. The nation implemented social policies to ensure equal opportunities, healthcare accessibility, and social protection for its citizens. Efforts were made to address issues such as poverty, unemployment, and inequality, with the aim of creating a more inclusive and cohesive society.

Malta's journey towards building a modern nation was intricately intertwined with its international relations and its role in the global community. The nation actively engaged in diplomatic efforts, forging alliances, and fostering partnerships with countries around the world. Membership in international organizations, such as the United Nations and the European Union, provided platforms for Malta to participate in global decision-making processes and contribute to shared goals.

The challenges faced by post-independence Malta were not without complexities and setbacks. The nation encountered obstacles ranging from economic recessions to social tensions and environmental concerns. However, the determination, resilience, and adaptability of the Maltese people enabled them to navigate these challenges and seize opportunities for progress.

Malta's strategic location in the Mediterranean continued to play a vital role in its post-independence trajectory. The nation's geostrategic position presented both opportunities and responsibilities in terms of regional security, migration management, and international cooperation. Malta embraced its role as a bridge between Europe, Africa, and the Middle East, fostering dialogue, promoting stability, and contributing to regional development efforts.

As Malta continues to navigate the complexities of the 21st century, the nation faces new challenges in areas such as sustainable development, technological advancements, climate change, and cultural preservation. These challenges provide opportunities for Malta to further strengthen its resilience, innovation, and commitment to a prosperous and harmonious future.

Malta in World War II: The Island's Heroic Resistance

World War II stands as one of the most tumultuous periods in human history, and for the small Mediterranean island of Malta, it was a time of immense challenges and heroic resistance. This chapter explores the remarkable story of Malta's role in World War II and the island's unwavering spirit in the face of relentless adversity.

Situated at a strategic crossroads between Europe and North Africa, Malta held significant strategic importance for both the Allies and the Axis powers. The island's deep-water harbors, airfields, and proximity to enemy supply lines made it a target for intense aerial bombardment and naval attacks.

In June 1940, Italy declared war on the Allies, and soon after, Malta became the target of sustained bombing raids by the Italian Air Force. The attacks aimed to neutralize the island's defenses, disrupt British operations in the Mediterranean, and pave the way for an invasion.

Despite being vastly outnumbered and outgunned, the people of Malta, along with the British and Commonwealth forces stationed on the island, displayed extraordinary resilience and determination. The Maltese population, which had already endured economic hardships and restrictions due to the war, now faced relentless bombardment, scarcity of supplies, and the constant threat of invasion.

The island's defense was bolstered by the Royal Air Force (RAF) and the Royal Navy, which provided crucial support and reinforcements. RAF squadrons based in Malta engaged in fierce aerial battles with the Axis forces, contesting control of the skies and preventing enemy air superiority.

The siege of Malta intensified when Germany entered the war in 1940. The Luftwaffe, the German air force, unleashed a relentless bombing campaign, subjecting the island to wave after wave of airstrikes. Malta became one of the most heavily bombed places on Earth, enduring constant bombardment for over two years.

The Maltese people, soldiers, and civilians alike, demonstrated remarkable bravery and resilience in the face of adversity. They endured the relentless onslaught, often sheltering in underground tunnels, caves, and improvised shelters to seek safety from the bombings. Despite the hardships, the morale remained remarkably high, with the people showing unwavering support for the Allied cause.

The bravery and sacrifices made during the siege of Malta earned the island the prestigious George Cross, a testament to the heroic resistance and the spirit of the Maltese people. The honor, awarded by King George VI of the United Kingdom, recognized the island's exceptional courage and determination.

The strategic importance of Malta in the Mediterranean eventually led to Operation Pedestal, a critical convoy mission aimed at resupplying the island. In August 1942, a convoy of Allied ships, protected by naval escorts and air cover, successfully fought its way through intense enemy attacks to deliver essential supplies to Malta. The convoy's success bolstered the island's defenses and provided a much-needed lifeline.

The resolute defense and the successful supply missions to Malta eventually turned the tide in favor of the Allies in the Mediterranean theater. The island's strategic position, along with the determined resistance of its people, disrupted enemy supply lines, forced the Axis powers to divert resources, and contributed to the ultimate victory of the Allied forces.

The heroic resistance and sacrifices made by the people of Malta during World War II hold a prominent place in the island's collective memory. The resilience, bravery, and unwavering spirit displayed during the siege are celebrated as a testament to the indomitable human spirit.

Maltese Culture and Identity: Language, Customs, and Traditions

Maltese culture is a rich tapestry woven from a diverse range of influences and traditions. The island's unique location at the crossroads of the Mediterranean has shaped its culture and identity, blending elements from various civilizations and creating a distinct Maltese heritage. This chapter explores the facets of Maltese culture, including language, customs, and traditions.

Language plays a vital role in shaping the cultural identity of a nation, and in Malta, the Maltese language holds a special place. Maltese is the official language of the island, spoken by the majority of the population. It is a Semitic language with a unique blend of influences, including Arabic, Italian, English, and French. The preservation of the Maltese language reflects the island's deep-rooted heritage and connection to its historical legacy.

Alongside Maltese, English is widely spoken and serves as the second official language. The bilingualism of the Maltese people is a testament to their cosmopolitan outlook and the nation's historical ties with the British Empire. The proficiency in English has also contributed to Malta's role as an international business and tourism hub.

Customs and traditions hold a significant place in Maltese culture, contributing to a strong sense of community and shared identity. The Maltese people have a deep respect for family values and the importance of close-knit relationships. Family gatherings, often centered around food and conversation, form an integral part of the Maltese way of life.

Religion, predominantly Roman Catholicism, has played a pivotal role in shaping Maltese customs and traditions. The influence of the Catholic Church can be seen in various aspects of Maltese life, from religious festivals and processions to the architectural beauty of churches and religious art. The devotion to religious practices and the celebration of feast days reflects the strong spiritual bond within the community.

One of the most vibrant aspects of Maltese culture is the celebration of traditional feasts, known as festi. Each village and town in Malta has its own patron saint, and throughout the year, these saints are honored with colorful processions, fireworks, music, and street decorations. Festi provide an opportunity for the community to come together, showcase their creativity, and express their deep-rooted traditions.

Malta's geographical location and seafaring history have influenced its culinary traditions. Maltese cuisine is a delicious blend of Mediterranean flavors, incorporating influences from Italy, North Africa, and the Middle East. Local ingredients such as fresh seafood, olives, tomatoes, and traditional pastries like pastizzi and qassatat contribute to the distinctive flavors of Maltese cuisine.

Music and folkloric dances also form an integral part of Maltese culture. Traditional music, including għana (Maltese folk music) and banda (brass band music), showcase the island's musical heritage. Folk dances, such as the Maltese Festa Dance and the Għana Dance, are performed during festive occasions, embodying the spirit and joy of the Maltese people.

Artistic expression is deeply rooted in Maltese culture. The islands have a rich artistic heritage, with influences ranging from ancient civilizations to contemporary trends. Traditional crafts, such as filigree jewelry, glassblowing, and lace-making, continue to thrive and showcase the craftsmanship of the Maltese people.

The natural beauty of Malta, with its picturesque landscapes, crystal-clear waters, and stunning architecture, has also inspired artists, writers, and filmmakers. The island has served as a backdrop for numerous international productions, further contributing to its cultural vibrancy and artistic legacy.

Exploring Malta's Countryside: Nature and Wildlife

Beyond its historical and cultural treasures, Malta is also home to breathtaking natural landscapes and a diverse array of wildlife. This chapter invites you to embark on a journey through Malta's countryside, exploring its natural beauty and discovering the unique flora and fauna that thrive on the islands.

Despite its small size, Malta boasts a surprising variety of natural landscapes. From rugged cliffs and dramatic coastlines to rolling hills and fertile valleys, the islands offer a rich tapestry of ecosystems to explore. The unique geology, shaped by millennia of volcanic activity and erosion, has given rise to stunning rock formations, caves, and natural harbors.

The Mediterranean climate, with its warm summers and mild winters, contributes to the flourishing of an abundance of plant life. Malta is home to over 1,000 species of plants, including endemic varieties found nowhere else in the world. The islands' diverse habitats, including garigue (low-growing vegetation), maquis (shrubland), and woodlands, provide niches for a wide range of plant species to thrive.

One iconic plant species synonymous with the Maltese countryside is the Maltese Rock Centaury (Cheirolophus crassifolius), which is endemic to the islands. This unique plant, with its vibrant purple flowers, can be found clinging to cliffs and rocky outcrops, adding a splash of color to the rugged landscape.

The Maltese countryside is also home to a remarkable array of wildlife, both on land and in the surrounding waters. The islands' strategic location along bird migration routes makes Malta a haven for birdwatching enthusiasts. Over 200 species of birds have been recorded, including migratory birds such as the Honey Buzzard, European Bee-eater, and various species of warblers.

The coastal areas and surrounding seas of Malta teem with marine life, offering opportunities for snorkeling, diving, and exploring underwater ecosystems. The crystal-clear waters reveal vibrant coral reefs, sea grass meadows, and a variety of fish species, including colorful wrasses, groupers, and damselfish.

Malta's countryside is also home to a range of terrestrial wildlife. The islands provide habitat for reptiles, such as the endemic Maltese Wall Lizard (Podarcis filfolensis), which can be spotted basking in the sun on rocky outcrops. Small mammals, such as hedgehogs and shrews, can be found in the rural areas, while bats inhabit the caves and old buildings.

In recent years, Malta has made efforts to preserve and protect its natural heritage. Several nature reserves and protected areas have been established to safeguard important habitats and species. These areas, such as Buskett Gardens, Ghadira Nature Reserve, and the island of Filfla, offer visitors the opportunity to experience the unspoiled beauty of Malta's countryside and observe its wildlife in their natural habitats.

Environmental organizations and government initiatives work together to promote sustainable practices and conservation efforts. Educational programs and awareness campaigns aim to foster a deeper appreciation for Malta's natural heritage and encourage responsible tourism.

As you venture into Malta's countryside, take the time to explore the scenic trails, discover hidden coves, and immerse yourself in the tranquility of nature. Whether it's observing a flock of migrating birds, marveling at the vibrant wildflowers, or diving into the crystal-clear waters to encounter marine life, Malta's natural wonders await your exploration.

The Azure Window and Natural Wonders of Malta

Malta is blessed with a plethora of natural wonders that captivate visitors from around the world. Among these, the Azure Window stood as a remarkable geological formation and a symbol of the island's scenic beauty. This chapter explores the Azure Window and other awe-inspiring natural wonders that grace the Maltese archipelago.

The Azure Window, also known as Tieqa tad-Dwejra in Maltese, was a natural limestone arch located on the island of Gozo. Over centuries, wind and water erosion sculpted this stunning formation, creating a window-like opening that offered breathtaking views of the surrounding sea. The Azure Window was an iconic landmark and a popular tourist attraction, drawing visitors to marvel at its majestic beauty.

Sadly, in 2017, the Azure Window succumbed to the forces of nature and collapsed during a severe storm. Its demise served as a reminder of the impermanence of natural formations and the need to appreciate and protect these wonders for future generations. While the physical structure of the Azure Window may no longer exist, its memory lives on as a testament to the island's natural splendor.

Beyond the Azure Window, Malta is home to an array of other natural wonders that continue to inspire awe and wonder. The Blue Grotto, located on the southern coast of Malta, is a series of sea caves renowned for their stunning azure waters. Visitors can explore these caves by boat, witnessing the interplay of light and water that creates an ethereal and magical experience.

The Dingli Cliffs, situated on the western coast of Malta, offer panoramic views of the Mediterranean Sea. These majestic limestone cliffs provide a dramatic backdrop for nature enthusiasts and photographers alike. The cliffs also serve as an important nesting site for various bird species, adding to the ecological significance of the area.

Malta's coastline is adorned with picturesque bays and hidden coves. Among these is the stunning Ramla Bay, located on the island of Gozo. With its golden-red sand, crystal-clear waters, and lush surroundings, Ramla Bay is considered one of the most beautiful beaches in the Mediterranean. It provides a tranquil escape and a perfect spot to soak in the natural beauty of the Maltese islands.

Inland, Malta is dotted with verdant valleys and fertile landscapes. Wied il-Għasri, a picturesque valley on Gozo, offers a serene retreat surrounded by cliffs and overlooking a narrow inlet. The valley is a haven for hikers, nature lovers, and those seeking solitude amidst the island's natural splendor.

Comino, the smallest inhabited island in the Maltese archipelago, is a haven for nature enthusiasts. The island's highlight is the Blue Lagoon, a mesmerizing lagoon with crystal-clear turquoise waters. It is a popular destination for swimming, snorkeling, and basking in the beauty of nature.

The natural wonders of Malta extend underwater as well. The islands are renowned for their rich marine life and vibrant coral reefs. Scuba diving and snorkeling enthusiasts can explore the underwater world teeming with colorful fish, seagrass meadows, and fascinating rock formations.

Malta's commitment to preserving its natural heritage is evident through the establishment of protected areas and nature reserves. These areas, such as the Dwejra Nature Reserve, Delimara Peninsula, and Foresta 2000, safeguard important habitats, endemic species, and migratory bird routes. They provide opportunities for visitors to connect with nature, witness wildlife in their natural habitats, and learn about the importance of conservation.

As you immerse yourself in the natural wonders of Malta, take the time to appreciate the delicate balance of ecosystems, the resilience of nature, and the breathtaking beauty that surrounds you. The Maltese archipelago offers a tapestry of landscapes, from majestic cliffs and azure waters to picturesque valleys and hidden bays. Embrace the opportunity to explore, respect, and preserve these natural treasures for future generations.

Maltese Cuisine: A Fusion of Mediterranean Flavors

Maltese cuisine is a delightful reflection of the island's rich history, cultural influences, and its unique position in the Mediterranean. This chapter takes you on a culinary journey through the vibrant and flavorful world of Maltese cuisine, showcasing the fusion of Mediterranean flavors that define its gastronomic identity.

Maltese cuisine draws inspiration from a diverse range of culinary traditions, blending elements from Mediterranean, Sicilian, North African, and Middle Eastern cuisines. This amalgamation of flavors creates a unique and tantalizing culinary experience that reflects the island's historical connections and its vibrant cultural tapestry.

One of the defining features of Maltese cuisine is its reliance on fresh and locally sourced ingredients. The island's fertile soil and Mediterranean climate provide an abundance of seasonal produce, which forms the backbone of many traditional dishes. Fresh vegetables, including tomatoes, peppers, eggplants, and zucchini, feature prominently in Maltese cooking, adding vibrant colors and flavors to the table.

Seafood holds a special place in Maltese cuisine, thanks to the island's proximity to the Mediterranean Sea. From succulent fish to shellfish delights, seafood is a highlight of many Maltese dishes. Local favorites include lampuki (dolphin fish), calamari (squid), and aljotta (fish soup). These dishes showcase the simplicity of preparation, allowing the natural flavors of the seafood to shine.

The use of herbs and spices adds depth and complexity to Maltese dishes. Basil, parsley, thyme, and mint are commonly used, infusing dishes with fresh and aromatic notes. The spice rack of a Maltese kitchen often includes cinnamon, cloves, nutmeg, and coriander, adding warmth and richness to stews, meat dishes, and pastries.

Bread holds a significant place in Maltese cuisine and is a staple at the Maltese table. Ftira, a traditional Maltese bread, is characterized by its round shape and chewy texture. It is often used as a base for delicious sandwiches, known as "hobz biz-zejt," which combine tomatoes, olive oil, garlic, capers, and tuna or anchovies. These sandwiches showcase the simplicity of Maltese cuisine while highlighting the quality of local ingredients.

Meat dishes are also prominent in Maltese cuisine, reflecting the influence of Mediterranean and North African culinary traditions. Fenek (rabbit) is a beloved and iconic Maltese dish, often stewed or roasted with garlic, wine, and herbs. Other popular meat dishes include lahmacun (minced meat pizza), beef stew, and roast pork.

Cheese plays a significant role in Maltese gastronomy. Ġbejna, a small round cheese made from sheep's or goat's milk, is a traditional Maltese cheese and a favorite among locals. It can be enjoyed fresh or aged, and its unique flavor adds a distinct touch to various dishes.

No exploration of Maltese cuisine would be complete without mentioning pastizzi. These delicious pastries, typically filled with either ricotta cheese or mushy peas, are a beloved Maltese street food. They are often enjoyed as a savory snack or for breakfast, accompanied by a cup of strong Maltese coffee.

Sweets and desserts hold a special place in Maltese cuisine, adding a delightful finale to a meal. Imqaret, sweet pastries filled with dates, are a traditional Maltese treat enjoyed during festive occasions. Kannoli, influenced by Sicilian cuisine, are crispy pastry tubes filled with sweet ricotta cream and often dusted with powdered sugar.

Maltese cuisine is not just about the dishes themselves; it encompasses the joy of sharing meals with loved ones and celebrating the island's vibrant culinary heritage. Family gatherings, feasts, and festive occasions provide opportunities to indulge in traditional flavors and create lasting memories.

As you explore the delectable world of Maltese cuisine, savor the harmony of flavors, the simplicity of preparation, and the pride that the Maltese people take in their culinary traditions. Allow your taste buds to be tantalized by the fusion of Mediterranean influences that have shaped the gastronomic identity of Malta.

The Maltese Language: A Unique Semitic Hybrid

The Maltese language stands as a remarkable linguistic phenomenon, embodying the history, culture, and identity of the Maltese people. As the only Semitic language written in Latin script, Maltese is a fusion of various influences, resulting in a unique linguistic hybrid that sets it apart from other languages. This chapter explores the fascinating intricacies of the Maltese language, its origins, structure, and significance in the Maltese society.

Maltese is the official language of Malta and is spoken by the majority of the population. It holds the distinction of being the only Semitic language in the European Union, making it a linguistically intriguing and culturally significant aspect of Malta's heritage.

The roots of the Maltese language can be traced back to the arrival of the Phoenicians, who established trading posts on the island around the 8th century BCE. The Phoenician influence laid the foundation for the Semitic character of the language, with many words and grammatical structures rooted in ancient Phoenician and Arabic.

Over the centuries, Malta's geographical location and historical interactions with various civilizations have contributed to the linguistic evolution of Maltese. The island has been influenced by Latin, Italian, Sicilian, French, and English, adding layers of vocabulary and linguistic patterns from these languages.

The result is a unique linguistic amalgamation where Semitic roots coexist with Romance and other European language elements. The lexical diversity of Maltese reflects this fusion, with words borrowed from Italian, French, and English, among others. This rich vocabulary contributes to the linguistic versatility of Maltese, allowing it to express a wide range of concepts and ideas.

The structure of the Maltese language follows a Semitic pattern, characterized by triconsonantal roots and a system of prefixes and suffixes. Verbs are conjugated according to tense, person, and number, while nouns have distinct forms for singular and plural. The grammatical structure of Maltese may present challenges for non-native speakers, but it showcases the linguistic heritage of the Maltese people.

The influence of the Arabic language on Maltese is particularly noteworthy. While Maltese is not mutually intelligible with Arabic, it shares significant lexical and grammatical similarities. Arabic loanwords in Maltese encompass various domains, including religion, food, and everyday expressions, adding depth to the linguistic tapestry.

The adoption of Latin script for writing Maltese differentiates it from other Semitic languages, which are typically written in Arabic script. The use of Latin script was introduced during the period of British colonial rule and has remained in use since then. This unique aspect allows for easier integration with European languages and facilitates written communication with non-Maltese speakers.

The preservation and promotion of the Maltese language have been essential components of Malta's cultural identity. The government has implemented policies to protect and nurture the language, including the establishment of language institutions, educational programs, and initiatives to encourage its use in various domains.

Language is an integral part of cultural heritage, and the Maltese language plays a vital role in shaping the identity of the Maltese people. It serves as a unifying force, connecting individuals to their roots and reinforcing a sense of belonging. The linguistic distinctiveness of Maltese adds richness and depth to the cultural fabric of Malta.

As you delve into the intricacies of the Maltese language, appreciate its uniqueness, and the fascinating blend of influences that have shaped its evolution. The linguistic heritage of Malta echoes the historical narrative of the island and serves as a testament to the resilience and adaptability of its people.

Valletta: The Fortress City and UNESCO World Heritage Site

Valletta, the capital city of Malta, stands as a testament to the island's rich history, architectural grandeur, and strategic significance. This chapter delves into the captivating story of Valletta, exploring its status as a fortress city and its well-deserved recognition as a UNESCO World Heritage Site.

Valletta was built on a peninsula in the northeast of Malta and holds the distinction of being one of the first planned cities in Europe. Its construction was initiated by Grand Master Jean de la Valette of the Order of St. John in the 16th century, following the successful defense of Malta during the Great Siege against the Ottoman Empire.

The city was meticulously designed by the renowned military architect Francesco Laparelli, who envisioned a fortified city that would serve as a stronghold against potential invaders. The layout of Valletta was carefully planned, featuring a grid system of streets that provided both defensive advantages and efficient urban organization.

The fortifications of Valletta are a hallmark of its architectural splendor. The massive bastions, strategically positioned along the city's walls, offer panoramic views of the surrounding harbors and the Mediterranean Sea. These fortifications, along with the imposing St. John's Co-Cathedral and other defensive structures, reflect the city's role as a formidable defense stronghold.

Valletta's architectural heritage is characterized by a blend of styles influenced by the various civilizations that have left their mark on Malta. The Baroque and Mannerist influences are particularly prominent, with ornate facades, grand palaces, and elegant churches adorning the cityscape. The iconic architecture of Valletta is a testament to the wealth and power of the Knights of St. John during their rule over the island.

St. John's Co-Cathedral stands as one of Valletta's most significant architectural treasures. This opulent cathedral, built between 1572 and 1577, showcases the artistic mastery of renowned artists, including Mattia Preti. The interior of the cathedral is adorned with intricate marble work, gilded details, and an impressive collection of paintings, including Caravaggio's masterpiece, "The Beheading of Saint John the Baptist."

Valletta's status as a UNESCO World Heritage Site is a testament to its outstanding universal value and the preservation efforts undertaken to protect its historical and cultural significance. The city's inclusion on the prestigious list acknowledges its exceptional urban planning, architectural splendor, and the tangible connections to Malta's unique historical narrative.

The streets of Valletta are steeped in history, lined with charming houses, quaint cafes, and bustling markets. The city's vibrant atmosphere, coupled with its rich cultural offerings, including museums, theaters, and art galleries, make it a hub of artistic and intellectual pursuits.

Valletta's strategic location and natural harbors have played a crucial role in Malta's maritime history. The Grand Harbor and Marsamxett Harbor continue to serve as bustling centers of trade and tourism, welcoming cruise ships and providing a gateway to the island's treasures.

Beyond its historical and architectural wonders, Valletta offers a vibrant and cosmopolitan lifestyle. The city hosts a multitude of events and festivals throughout the year, including the renowned Valletta Carnival and the Malta International Arts Festival. These celebrations showcase the city's cultural vibrancy and its ability to embrace both tradition and innovation.

Valletta's allure extends beyond its fortified walls, with panoramic views of the surrounding sea and the neighboring towns of Sliema and Floriana. The Upper Barrakka Gardens, perched atop the city's bastions, offer a tranquil retreat where visitors can enjoy stunning vistas and appreciate the city's strategic positioning.

As you explore Valletta's enchanting streets, immerse yourself in its history, and marvel at the architectural splendor that has withstood the test of time. The city's designation as a UNESCO World Heritage Site underscores its exceptional value and serves as a reminder of Malta's rich cultural legacy.

Mdina: The Silent City of Malta

Nestled in the heart of Malta, the ancient city of Mdina stands as a living testament to the island's storied past and architectural grandeur. Known as the Silent City, Mdina exudes an aura of tranquility and a sense of stepping back in time. This chapter unveils the captivating story of Mdina, exploring its historical significance, cultural heritage, and enduring allure.

Mdina's origins can be traced back to the Phoenician era, making it one of the oldest inhabited cities in Malta. Over the centuries, it has been shaped by the influence of various civilizations, including the Phoenicians, Romans, Arabs, and Knights of St. John. The city's strategic hilltop location provided a vantage point for observing potential invaders and defending the island.

The name "Mdina" is derived from the Arabic word "medina," meaning "walled city." This aptly describes the city's character, as Mdina is enclosed within impressive fortifications that have withstood the test of time. The imposing walls and gates, such as the majestic Main Gate and the striking Greeks' Gate, evoke a sense of stepping into a bygone era.

Entering Mdina is like stepping into a living museum, where every corner tells a story. The city's narrow, winding streets are lined with palaces, churches, and noble residences, showcasing a rich architectural heritage that spans centuries. The intricate details of the medieval facades, the ornate balconies, and the charming courtyards transport visitors to a world of timeless elegance.

One of Mdina's most iconic landmarks is the Cathedral of St. Paul, also known as Mdina Cathedral. This magnificent Baroque-style cathedral, dedicated to the Apostle Paul, dominates the city's skyline. Its opulent interior houses artistic treasures, including intricate marble work, stunning frescoes, and a magnificent gilded coffered ceiling.

Mdina's allure extends beyond its architectural splendor. The city offers breathtaking panoramic views of the surrounding landscapes, including the picturesque Maltese countryside and the distant Mediterranean Sea. The Bastions, located along the fortified walls, provide unparalleled vistas, particularly during sunset, when the golden hues bathe the city in a magical light.

The Silent City nickname is not merely a poetic description; it reflects the peaceful ambiance that pervades Mdina. Unlike the bustling streets of Valletta and other urban areas, Mdina's limited vehicular access contributes to a serene atmosphere. The absence of cars and the cobbled streets create a sense of timelessness and tranquility, allowing visitors to immerse themselves in the city's ambiance.

Mdina's cultural heritage is celebrated through various events and traditions. The annual Medieval Mdina Festival takes visitors on a journey back in time, with reenactments, music, and performances that transport them to the medieval era. The feast of St. Peter and St. Paul, celebrated on June 29th, brings the city to life with religious processions, colorful decorations, and vibrant festivities.

Mdina's charm has not gone unnoticed by the film industry. The city has served as a backdrop for numerous movies and TV productions, with its ancient walls and timeless atmosphere lending an air of authenticity to historical dramas and epic tales.

Mdina's enduring allure has made it a popular destination for visitors seeking to experience Malta's rich history and immerse themselves in a city frozen in time. Its historical significance, cultural heritage, and architectural splendor have earned it the status of a national monument and a key attraction within Malta's tourism landscape.

As you wander through the streets of Mdina, let yourself be transported to a world of knights, merchants, and nobles. Discover the hidden gems tucked away within its walls, savor the captivating views, and appreciate the sense of peace that envelops the Silent City.

The Three Cities: Vittoriosa, Senglea, and Cospicua

Situated on the southeastern coast of Malta, the Three Cities—Vittoriosa, Senglea, and Cospicua—stand as a testament to the island's maritime heritage, resilience, and architectural splendor. This chapter unveils the captivating story of these historic cities, exploring their significance, cultural heritage, and enduring charm.

Vittoriosa, also known as Birgu, is the oldest of the Three Cities and holds a special place in Malta's history. It served as the first capital of the Knights of St. John after their arrival in Malta in 1530. Vittoriosa's strategic location along the Grand Harbor made it a vital stronghold and an important center for trade and maritime activities.

Walking through the streets of Vittoriosa is like stepping back in time, with its well-preserved medieval architecture and narrow winding alleys. The city's fortified walls, bastions, and impressive fortresses, such as Fort St. Angelo, stand as a testament to its defensive significance and the prowess of the Knights of St. John.

Senglea, also known as L-Isla, sits opposite Vittoriosa and shares a similar historical and cultural legacy. The city was named after the Grand Master Claude de la Sengle, who fortified it during the 16th century. Senglea's location on a narrow peninsula allowed for better control of the harbor entrance and provided additional protection against potential invaders.

The streets of Senglea are steeped in history, lined with traditional townhouses adorned with colorful balconies. The city's urban fabric showcases architectural styles influenced by various periods, including the medieval, Baroque, and British colonial eras. Senglea's compact layout and charming ambiance make it a delight to explore on foot, with surprises around every corner.

Cospicua, also known as Bormla, completes the trio of the Three Cities. Like its neighboring cities, Cospicua played a pivotal role in Malta's maritime history. Its waterfront location and natural harbor, known as Dockyard Creek, made it a bustling center for shipbuilding, trade, and naval activities.

Cospicua's architecture reflects the influences of different periods, including the Baroque, British colonial, and Art Nouveau styles. The city's imposing churches, ornate facades, and picturesque squares create a captivating atmosphere. The Cottonera Lines, a series of fortifications that encircle the city, are a remarkable example of military engineering and highlight the strategic importance of Cospicua.

The Three Cities collectively bear witness to Malta's historical struggles and triumphs. These cities withstood sieges, attacks, and invasions, leaving behind a rich tapestry of stories and a deep sense of resilience. Their streets echo the footsteps of knights, sailors, and merchants who shaped the island's destiny.

Today, the Three Cities offer a fascinating blend of historical significance and modern vibrancy. The revitalization efforts undertaken in recent years have breathed new life into these cities, with the restoration of historic buildings, the emergence of boutique hotels, and the establishment of cultural and artistic spaces.

Exploring the Three Cities allows visitors to immerse themselves in Malta's maritime legacy and experience the charm of these historic enclaves. From the majestic forts and churches to the picturesque waterfront promenades, there is an abundance of architectural gems and hidden corners waiting to be discovered.

The Three Cities are not just repositories of history and architecture; they are also home to a tight-knit community proud of their heritage. Traditional feasts, religious processions, and cultural events showcase the vibrant spirit and sense of community that define these cities.

As you wander through the Three Cities, allow yourself to be transported back in time and appreciate the unique character of each city. The interconnectedness of Vittoriosa, Senglea, and Cospicua offers a comprehensive glimpse into Malta's maritime legacy and the indomitable spirit of its people.

The Hypogeum of Hal-Saflieni: An Ancient Underground Temple

Deep beneath the surface of Malta lies a remarkable archaeological treasure, the Hypogeum of Hal-Saflieni. This subterranean complex, dating back over 5,000 years, stands as a testament to the ingenuity and spiritual beliefs of Malta's prehistoric inhabitants. This chapter unveils the captivating story of the Hypogeum, exploring its historical significance, architectural marvels, and the mysteries that continue to surround this ancient underground temple.

The Hypogeum is located in the town of Paola, on the southeastern coast of Malta. Its discovery in 1902 by construction workers marked a pivotal moment in Malta's archaeological history. The site's significance was immediately recognized, and extensive excavations and preservation efforts have taken place to uncover its secrets and ensure its long-term preservation.

This underground complex is a testament to the advanced engineering skills of Malta's prehistoric societies. Carved out of solid limestone, the Hypogeum consists of three levels, each containing a network of interconnected chambers, corridors, and chambers. The precision and craftsmanship of the stone-cutting techniques are awe-inspiring, with walls, ceilings, and altars exhibiting meticulous attention to detail.

The Hypogeum's purpose remains a subject of intrigue and speculation among archaeologists and historians. The prevailing theory suggests that it served as a burial site and a place of ritual and worship. The lowermost level, known as the Holy of Holies, is believed to have held sacred artifacts and hosted religious ceremonies.

One of the most striking features of the Hypogeum is its acoustic properties. The architecture of the underground chambers creates a unique resonance and amplification of sound. The Oracle Room, in particular, is renowned for its remarkable acoustic capabilities, with whispers and sounds reverberating throughout the space. The intentional design of these acoustic effects underscores the importance of sound and ritualistic practices within the Hypogeum.

The walls of the Hypogeum are adorned with intricate carvings and paintings, providing insights into the spiritual beliefs and rituals of Malta's prehistoric inhabitants. These decorative motifs depict various anthropomorphic figures, animals, and geometric patterns, reflecting a connection to nature and a belief in the divine.

The preservation of the Hypogeum presents ongoing challenges due to its unique underground environment. The delicate balance of humidity, temperature, and airflow requires careful monitoring and conservation measures to prevent deterioration and maintain its structural integrity. As a result, visitor access to the Hypogeum is limited to preserve its fragile condition.

Due to its significance, the Hypogeum of Hal-Saflieni has been recognized as a UNESCO World Heritage Site since 1980. Its inclusion on this prestigious list acknowledges its outstanding universal value and the need for its protection and preservation for future generations.

Visiting the Hypogeum is an immersive experience that transports visitors to a distant past and offers a glimpse into the spiritual and cultural practices of Malta's prehistoric inhabitants. The careful management of visitor numbers and the guided tours provide an opportunity to appreciate the site's historical and archaeological significance.

The Hypogeum of Hal-Saflieni continues to enthrall researchers and visitors alike, as new discoveries and studies shed light on its enigmatic past. Its intricate architecture, mysterious purpose, and exceptional preservation make it a testament to the ingenuity and spiritual beliefs of Malta's ancient civilizations.

Gozo: The Sister Island of Maltese Legends

Just a short ferry ride away from mainland Malta lies the enchanting island of Gozo. Known as the sister island, Gozo boasts a distinct character, breathtaking landscapes, and a rich tapestry of legends and folklore. This chapter unravels the captivating story of Gozo, exploring its historical significance, natural wonders, and the enduring allure that has made it a beloved destination for locals and visitors alike.

Gozo, which means "joy" in Maltese, is the second-largest island in the Maltese archipelago. Its smaller size and slower pace of life offer a tranquil and idyllic escape from the bustling energy of Malta. Gozo's rural charm, unspoiled coastline, and picturesque villages exude a sense of timeless beauty.

The history of Gozo stretches back thousands of years. Archaeological evidence suggests that the island was inhabited since Neolithic times, and it has been influenced by various civilizations, including the Phoenicians, Romans, Arabs, and Knights of St. John. The remnants of these civilizations can still be seen today in the form of ancient temples, fortifications, and other architectural marvels.

Gozo's landscape is a captivating blend of rolling hills, fertile valleys, and dramatic cliffs that plunge into the azure Mediterranean Sea. The island's rugged coastline is dotted with secluded coves, pristine beaches, and hidden caves, inviting visitors to explore its natural wonders. The famous

Azure Window, a natural limestone arch that once graced Gozo's coast, sadly collapsed in 2017, but the island still boasts numerous breathtaking viewpoints and picturesque coastal vistas.

The charming villages of Gozo are steeped in history and brimming with authentic Maltese character. Victoria, also known as Rabat, serves as the island's capital and cultural hub. Its centerpiece is the imposing Citadel, a fortified city perched atop a hill that offers panoramic views of the surrounding countryside. The Citadel has witnessed the passage of time and serves as a reminder of Gozo's strategic significance throughout history.

Gozo's religious devotion is evident in its numerous churches, chapels, and shrines, which dot the landscape. The majestic Basilica of the National Shrine of the Blessed Virgin of Ta' Pinu holds a special place in the hearts of the Maltese people, drawing pilgrims from near and far to pay homage to the island's beloved patroness.

Legend and folklore play a significant role in Gozo's cultural heritage. The island is steeped in mythical tales, from the enchanting story of the nymph Calypso, who, according to Homer's Odyssey, held Odysseus captive on Gozo, to the legends of giants and mystical creatures that roam its hills and valleys. These legends add a touch of mysticism and wonder to the island's already captivating allure.

Gozo's rural character and fertile land contribute to its reputation as an agricultural hub. The island is renowned for its fresh produce, including sun-ripened tomatoes, juicy melons, and flavorful cheeses. Visitors can indulge in the island's culinary delights, savoring the taste of locally sourced ingredients and traditional Maltese dishes.

Gozo's laid-back ambiance and natural beauty have made it a haven for artists, writers, and those seeking creative inspiration. The island's charming villages, rugged landscapes, and picturesque seascapes have provided a backdrop for numerous artistic endeavors, capturing the hearts and imaginations of those who visit.

Gozo's cultural calendar is brimming with events and festivals that celebrate the island's heritage. The annual Santa Marija feast, held in August, is a highlight, attracting locals and tourists alike with its colorful processions, fireworks displays, and lively street celebrations.

The warm hospitality of the Gozitan people is an integral part of the island's charm. Visitors are welcomed with open arms and are invited to immerse themselves in the local way of life, from exploring traditional craft markets to sampling Gozitan delicacies at family-run restaurants.

The Blue Grotto and the Mysteries of the Sea

Perched on the southern coast of Malta lies a natural wonder that has captivated visitors for centuries—the Blue Grotto. This enchanting sea cave complex, with its vibrant azure waters and breathtaking rock formations, beckons adventurers and nature lovers to explore its hidden depths. In this chapter, we delve into the mysteries of the sea and the allure of the Blue Grotto, uncovering its geological wonders, marine life, and the magical experiences it offers.

The Blue Grotto is located near the village of Żurrieq and is accessible by boat from the nearby fishing village of Wied iż-Żurrieq. Its name is derived from the brilliant blue hue that illuminates the cave interiors when sunlight penetrates the crystal-clear waters, creating an ethereal and mesmerizing spectacle.

The complex comprises a series of seven sea caves carved out by the relentless action of the sea against the limestone cliffs over thousands of years. Each cave has its own unique characteristics, with intricate rock formations that have been shaped by the forces of nature. The largest and most impressive cave is known as the Blue Grotto, drawing the majority of visitors to its awe-inspiring beauty.

Exploring the Blue Grotto is a truly immersive experience. Visitors embark on small boats operated by experienced local boatmen who skillfully navigate the caves, showcasing their intimate knowledge of the sea's currents and tides. As the boat glides through the entrance of the cave, visitors are enveloped in a world of striking blue hues, with sunlight dancing on the water's surface and illuminating the limestone walls.

The phenomenon of the Blue Grotto's vibrant blue coloration is attributed to the interplay of natural light, the unique properties of the water, and the reflection and refraction of sunlight. The sunlight enters the caves through various openings and interacts with the water and the cave walls, resulting in a mesmerizing display of blue hues that range from deep sapphire to electric turquoise.

The Blue Grotto is not just a visual wonder; it also harbors a rich marine ecosystem. Beneath the surface, the waters teem with life, showcasing a diverse array of marine species. Snorkelers and scuba divers can explore the underwater world, encountering colorful fish, vibrant coral formations, and even the occasional sighting of octopuses and other fascinating marine creatures.

The waters surrounding the Blue Grotto are part of a protected marine area, ensuring the conservation and preservation of the delicate ecosystem. The responsible management of the site aims to maintain the balance between tourism and environmental sustainability, allowing visitors to appreciate its beauty while safeguarding its natural heritage.

The Blue Grotto's allure extends beyond its stunning visuals and marine life. It has become an iconic symbol of Malta's natural beauty and a popular destination for artists, photographers, and nature enthusiasts seeking inspiration and a sense of tranquility. The interplay of light and color, the intricate rock formations, and the ever-changing reflections create a kaleidoscope of sensory experiences that are truly unforgettable.

Visiting the Blue Grotto is subject to weather conditions and sea state, as the safety of visitors is paramount. It is advisable to check with local authorities or boat operators before planning a visit to ensure the best possible experience.

St. John's Co-Cathedral: Baroque Splendor in Valletta

In the heart of Malta's capital city, Valletta, stands a masterpiece of Baroque architecture and religious grandeur—St. John's Co-Cathedral. This chapter unveils the captivating story of this architectural gem, exploring its historical significance, artistic treasures, and the awe-inspiring atmosphere that has made it a cultural and spiritual landmark.

St. John's Co-Cathedral was built between 1572 and 1577 by the Knights of St. John, also known as the Knights Hospitaller. The construction of the cathedral was prompted by the need for a grand place of worship for the order, as well as a symbol of their power and devotion.

The cathedral's facade, although relatively modest compared to its opulent interior, displays a classical design with a prominent doorway and tall windows. It gives little indication of the grandeur that lies beyond its doors.

Upon entering St. John's Co-Cathedral, visitors are immediately transported into a world of breathtaking beauty and artistic splendor. The interior of the cathedral is a masterful example of Baroque architecture, adorned with intricate details, gilded decorations, and awe-inspiring works of art.

The most renowned feature of the cathedral is its richly decorated marble floor, consisting of more than 400 tombstones commemorating the knights and other distinguished individuals. The mosaic patterns and designs are a testament to the exquisite craftsmanship and attention to detail.

The artistic treasures of St. John's Co-Cathedral extend beyond the floor. The cathedral houses a remarkable collection of paintings by renowned artists of the time, including Caravaggio's masterpiece, "The Beheading of St. John the Baptist." Caravaggio's painting, known for its dramatic lighting and intense realism, is considered one of the artist's greatest works and a highlight of the cathedral's art collection.

The chapels within St. John's Co-Cathedral showcase a fusion of architectural styles and decorative elements. Each chapel tells its own story and pays tribute to the different nationalities and noble families associated with the Knights of St. John. From the ornate Chapel of the Langue of Aragon to the grand Chapel of the Langue of Italy, each space is a testament to the wealth and power of the order and its benefactors.

The cathedral's ornate altar, adorned with gilded decorations and intricate carvings, is the focal point of the main sanctuary. It exudes a sense of grandeur and provides a space for contemplation and worship.

St. John's Co-Cathedral's architectural and artistic significance is further elevated by its role as a co-cathedral. Although the cathedral shares this status with the Cathedral of the Assumption in Mdina, it serves as the primary seat of the Archbishop of Malta.

Visiting St. John's Co-Cathedral allows visitors to immerse themselves in the history and artistry of the Knights of St. John. The cathedral provides a glimpse into the grandeur and devotion of the order, showcasing their legacy as defenders of the Catholic faith and their patron saint, St. John the Baptist.

The ongoing preservation efforts and restoration work undertaken at St. John's Co-Cathedral ensure its continued splendor for future generations to appreciate. The cathedral's significance has been recognized by UNESCO, which included it as part of the "City of Valletta" World Heritage Site in 1980.

Stepping out of St. John's Co-Cathedral, visitors can't help but feel a sense of awe and reverence for the artistry, history, and spiritual significance it embodies. The Baroque splendor and meticulous craftsmanship serve as a testament to the enduring legacy of the Knights of St. John and their contribution to Malta's cultural heritage.

The Malta Experience: A Multimedia Journey through History

When it comes to unraveling the captivating history of Malta, there is one immersive and educational experience that stands out—the Malta Experience. This multimedia journey takes visitors on a captivating voyage through time, providing insights into the island's rich heritage, cultural significance, and historical milestones. In this chapter, we delve into the Malta Experience, exploring its unique approach, technological innovations, and the enriching experience it offers to visitors.

The Malta Experience is located in Valletta, Malta's capital city, and serves as a gateway to understanding the island's past. The experience combines audiovisual presentations, stunning visuals, and captivating storytelling to create a multi-sensory journey that engages visitors of all ages.

The journey begins in a purpose-built theater equipped with state-of-the-art technology. As visitors settle into their seats, the lights dim, and the immersive experience begins. The theater's large screen, surround sound system, and special effects transport the audience to different periods in Malta's history, from prehistoric times to the present day.

The narrative unfolds through a combination of expertly crafted storytelling, historical reenactments, and captivating visuals. Through the use of high-definition projections, visitors are immersed in the sights and sounds of significant events, such as the Great Siege of Malta, the building of Valletta, and the island's struggles and triumphs.

The Malta Experience goes beyond mere historical retelling; it aims to create an emotional connection with the audience. The audiovisual presentations are complemented by a powerful soundtrack that evokes the mood and atmosphere of each historical period. Visitors can't help but be drawn into the narrative, feeling the triumphs, sorrows, and resilience of the Maltese people throughout history.

One of the highlights of the Malta Experience is its commitment to historical accuracy. The content is thoroughly researched and reviewed by historians and experts in Maltese history, ensuring that the information presented is reliable and factual. Visitors can trust that they are gaining a true understanding of Malta's past, free from embellishments or fictional elements.

The Malta Experience also offers a valuable educational resource for schools and students. The interactive nature of the experience, combined with its engaging presentations, makes it an effective tool for teaching history to younger generations. It brings the past to life, fostering a deeper understanding and appreciation for the island's heritage.

The success of the Malta Experience lies in its ability to make history accessible and enjoyable for a wide range of visitors. Its engaging approach transcends language barriers, as the presentations are available in multiple languages, allowing visitors from different countries to fully immerse themselves in the journey.

The Malta Experience is not just a passive viewing experience; it also provides an opportunity for visitors to delve deeper into specific aspects of Malta's history. The on-site exhibition offers additional information, artifacts, and interactive displays that allow visitors to engage with the content on a more personal level.

The experience is a testament to the technological advancements in the field of multimedia storytelling. The use of high-definition projections, surround sound, and special effects creates a truly immersive and memorable experience. It showcases the power of technology in enhancing our understanding and appreciation of history.

For those seeking to deepen their understanding of Malta's rich heritage, the Malta Experience provides a comprehensive and engaging journey through time. It ignites curiosity, sparks the imagination, and fosters a greater appreciation for the island's cultural significance and historical legacy.

The Malta Maritime Museum: Tales of the Sea

In the historic coastal city of Birgu, nestled within the ancient Fort St. Angelo, lies a treasure trove of maritime history—the Malta Maritime Museum. This chapter takes us on a fascinating journey through the museum's halls, exploring the captivating tales of the sea, the island's maritime heritage, and the invaluable artifacts that tell the story of Malta's seafaring past.

The Malta Maritime Museum is housed in a former naval bakery within the formidable walls of Fort St. Angelo, which has played a crucial role in Malta's maritime history. The museum itself was established in 1992, with the aim of preserving and showcasing Malta's rich nautical heritage.

Upon entering the museum, visitors are greeted by a diverse collection of artifacts, exhibits, and interactive displays that offer a comprehensive overview of Malta's maritime traditions. The exhibits are thoughtfully organized and curated, allowing visitors to delve into different aspects of maritime history, from shipbuilding and navigation to naval warfare and trade.

One of the focal points of the museum is its collection of model ships, which range from intricate replicas of ancient vessels to detailed representations of majestic warships. These models provide a glimpse into the evolution of shipbuilding techniques, the diversity of vessels that once sailed Malta's waters, and the importance of maritime trade and exploration.

As visitors wander through the museum, they encounter artifacts and memorabilia that offer insights into the daily lives of seafarers and the challenges they faced. From navigational instruments and tools to personal belongings of sailors, each item tells a unique story and adds depth to the narrative of Malta's maritime history.

The museum also pays tribute to Malta's naval prowess and its role in defending the island's shores throughout history. The collection includes weaponry, cannons, and armor that highlight the military aspect of maritime heritage. These artifacts serve as a reminder of the strategic importance of Malta's position in the Mediterranean and the resilience of its people in safeguarding their homeland.

In addition to the permanent exhibits, the Malta Maritime Museum regularly hosts temporary exhibitions and special events, offering a dynamic and ever-evolving experience for visitors. These exhibitions may focus on specific themes, such as underwater archaeology or the exploration of Malta's submarine heritage, further enriching the museum's offerings.

The museum's educational initiatives are also noteworthy. It provides educational programs and workshops for schools and engages with the local community through outreach activities. These initiatives aim to foster a deeper understanding and appreciation for Malta's maritime heritage, ensuring its preservation for future generations.

The Malta Maritime Museum's location within Fort St. Angelo adds another layer of historical significance to the experience. The fort, with its imposing presence and strategic position overlooking the Grand Harbor, has witnessed centuries of naval activity and played a pivotal role in the island's maritime defense.

Stepping out of the Malta Maritime Museum, visitors gain a renewed appreciation for the profound influence of the sea on Malta's history, culture, and identity. The museum's comprehensive collection and engaging exhibits offer a window into the island's seafaring past, reminding us of the vital role that maritime activities have played in shaping Malta's destiny.

The preservation of Malta's maritime heritage is an ongoing endeavor, and the Malta Maritime Museum serves as a vital custodian of this legacy. Through its exhibits, educational programs, and community engagement, the museum ensures that the tales of the sea continue to be told, celebrated, and cherished.

From Megaliths to Modernity: Malta's Enduring Legacy

As our journey through Malta's captivating history comes to a close, we reflect on the island's enduring legacy—a testament to the resilience, creativity, and cultural richness of its people. From the enigmatic megalithic temples to the architectural marvels of Valletta, and from the tumultuous times of invasion and siege to the modern developments of the 21st century, Malta has carved its place in the annals of human history.

The megalithic temples of Malta stand as awe-inspiring reminders of the island's ancient past. Dating back over 5,000 years, these prehistoric structures predate the pyramids of Egypt and Stonehenge in the United Kingdom. The temples, such as Ħaġar Qim, Mnajdra, and Tarxien, are testimony to the advanced architectural skills and spiritual beliefs of Malta's earliest inhabitants. Their construction techniques, precise alignments with celestial phenomena, and intricate carvings continue to intrigue archaeologists and visitors alike.

The influence of various civilizations has shaped Malta's history and left an indelible mark on its cultural heritage. The Phoenicians, Romans, Byzantines, Arabs, and Knights of St. John all made their mark on the island, contributing to its rich tapestry of traditions, customs, and architectural marvels. The fusion of these influences has resulted in a unique and vibrant Maltese identity that celebrates diversity and embraces its multicultural past.

The medieval period brought both challenges and triumphs for Malta. The arrival of the Knights Templar and later the Knights of St. John ushered in an era of grandeur and prosperity. The construction of fortifications, such as Fort St. Angelo, Fort St. Elmo, and the city of Mdina, transformed Malta into a formidable stronghold and a key player in the Mediterranean theater. The Great Siege of Malta in 1565, where the Knights successfully repelled the Ottoman Empire, stands as a testament to the island's resilience and strategic importance.

The legacy of the Knights of St. John is intertwined with the architectural splendor of Valletta, the capital city of Malta. Designed by the renowned architect Francesco Laparelli, Valletta was built as a fortified city and named after Grand Master Jean de Valette, who led the defense against the Ottomans. The city's grid-like layout, Baroque architecture, and grand palaces, including the Auberge de Castille and the Grandmaster's Palace, showcase the opulence and power of the Knights. Valletta was designated a UNESCO World Heritage Site in 1980, acknowledging its outstanding universal value.

British rule in Malta, which lasted from 1800 to 1964, brought significant changes to the island's infrastructure, education, and governance. Under British administration, Malta experienced modernization and economic development. The construction of major public works, such as the Victoria Lines and the Malta Railway, transformed the island's transportation system. The British also left a lasting influence on Malta's legal system, education system, and language, with English becoming an official language alongside Maltese.

Malta's journey to independence and the subsequent challenges of building a modern nation marked another chapter in its history. In 1964, Malta gained independence from British rule and embarked on a path of self-governance. The island faced economic and social transformations, navigating its way through the complexities of international relations, embracing European integration, and adapting to a globalized world.

Today, Malta stands as a thriving European nation, blending its historical legacy with modernity. Its strategic location in the Mediterranean, vibrant cultural scene, and robust economy make it a hub for tourism, finance, and digital innovation. The island's commitment to preserving its heritage is evident in its ongoing restoration projects, museum initiatives, and the safeguarding of its architectural gems.

From megaliths to modernity, Malta's enduring legacy is a testament to the resilience, creativity, and adaptability of its people. The island's rich history, cultural diversity, and remarkable treasures continue to captivate visitors from around the world. As we conclude our exploration of Malta's captivating narrative, we leave with a deep appreciation for the island's remarkable journey through time and the enduring spirit that shapes its trajectory.

Conclusion

Our exploration of Malta's captivating history has taken us on a remarkable journey through time, unearthing the island's rich heritage, cultural tapestry, and architectural marvels. From the enigmatic megalithic temples that predate the pyramids to the grandeur of Valletta's Baroque architecture, and from the heroic resistance against invasions to the modern developments of the 21st century, Malta's story is one of resilience, diversity, and enduring legacy.

The history of Malta is a testament to the strategic importance of its location in the heart of the Mediterranean. Over the centuries, various civilizations and empires sought to claim the island for its advantageous position, resulting in a rich tapestry of influences that have shaped its culture, language, and architecture.

The megalithic temples, such as Ħaġar Qim and Mnajdra, stand as mysterious remnants of Malta's prehistoric past. These impressive structures, crafted with remarkable precision and aligned with celestial phenomena, provide a glimpse into the spiritual beliefs and advanced architectural skills of Malta's earliest inhabitants.

The Phoenicians, Romans, Byzantines, Arabs, and Knights of St. John all left their mark on Malta, contributing to its cultural mosaic. Each civilization brought with it its own traditions, customs, and architectural styles, creating a unique blend that defines Malta's identity today.

The era of the Knights of St. John stands out as a golden age in Malta's history. Their arrival in the 16th century transformed the island into a formidable stronghold and a center of cultural and artistic excellence. The grand fortifications, palaces, and churches they built, such as St. John's Co-Cathedral and the Auberge de Castille, continue to captivate visitors with their opulence and grandeur.

Malta's strategic significance in the Mediterranean was demonstrated during the Great Siege of 1565 when the Knights successfully defended the island against the might of the Ottoman Empire. This pivotal event in Malta's history showcased the resilience and determination of its people, solidifying the island's reputation as a key player in the region.

British rule, which lasted from 1800 to 1964, brought significant changes to Malta's infrastructure and governance. The British left a lasting influence on the island's legal system, education, and language, with English becoming an official language alongside Maltese.

Malta's journey to independence marked a new chapter in its history. Since gaining independence in 1964, the island has navigated its way through economic and social transformations, embracing European integration, and adapting to the challenges and opportunities of the modern world.

Today, Malta is a thriving European nation that blends its historical legacy with modernity. Its strategic location, vibrant cultural scene, and robust economy make it a sought-after destination for tourism, business, and innovation. The preservation of its architectural heritage, the promotion of its cultural richness, and the commitment to sustainable development ensure that Malta's legacy will continue to be celebrated and cherished.

As we conclude our exploration of Malta's captivating narrative, we leave with a deep appreciation for the island's remarkable journey through time. From ancient civilizations to modernity, Malta's enduring legacy is a testament to the resilience, creativity, and adaptability of its people. The treasures we have uncovered, the stories we have unraveled, and the diverse influences that have shaped Malta's identity invite us to embrace the richness of this extraordinary island.

May the knowledge gained from our exploration inspire further appreciation and curiosity about Malta's history, culture, and heritage. As we bid farewell to this captivating journey, we carry with us the enduring spirit of Malta and the lessons learned from its remarkable past.

Thank you for embarking on this fascinating journey through the history of Malta with me. I hope that the chapters have transported you to the ancient temples, fortified cities, and grand cathedrals that embody the island's rich heritage. It has been a pleasure to guide you through the captivating stories, cultural treasures, and remarkable landmarks that make Malta truly extraordinary.

Your support and interest in this book are greatly appreciated. If you have enjoyed this exploration of Malta's history and found it informative and engaging, I kindly request that you consider leaving a positive review. Your feedback will not only encourage other readers to embark on this journey but also inspire me to continue creating captivating content.

Once again, thank you for your time, curiosity, and support. It has been an honor to share the stories of Malta's past, and I hope they have left a lasting impression. Your positive review will not only brighten my day but also contribute to the success of this book.

www.ingramcontent.com/pod-product-compliance
Ingram Content Group UK Ltd.
Pitfield, Milton Keynes, MK11 3LW, UK
UKHW021458300125
4369UKWH00043B/695

9 798850 013646